DRAWINGS
OF THE HOLBEIN FAMILY

Chosen and edited by Edmund Schilling

61 Plates
after drawings by Hans Holbein the Elder
and his sons Ambrosius Holbein and Hans Holbein the Younger

THE ART BOOK PUBLICATIONS
251 West 57th Street · New York

Printed in Belgium
Translated by Eveline Byam Shaw
All Rights Reserved
1939

Plates Nos. 21-56 have been made with the help of : P. Ganz, *Die Handzeichnungen Hans Holbeins des Jüngeren*, 40 Parts, in 8 volumes, Berlin and Basle 1910-26.—Reference was also made, with the kind permission of the author, to the Critical Catalogue at present in the press.

ARTISTS' STUDIOS of the late Middle Ages were often the common work shops of single families. A painter's brothers and sons worked under his direction —each according to his capabilities. While the more modest talents fulfilled whatever task was set them, clinging as closely as possible to the familiar style of the studio, the more independant spirits strove towards an unrestrained and individual activity.

The history of Hans Holbein the Elder and his sons, occuring in the transition period from Gothic to Renaissance, is readily accessible to us, for a lucky fate has preserved a large quantity of records, paintings and drawings.

Hans Holbein the Elder was born at Augsburg beween 1460 and 1470. After travels which took him to the Netherlands by way of Ulm, he settled in Augsburg in 1493.

The artist must soon have found recognition. It was at the beginning of the 16th century that he painted most of those pictures, to be found to-day in public collections, the great series of pictures from the Passion, the Life of the Virgin, and Stories of the Saints : in 1501 the High Altar of the Dominican Church at Frankfort, in 1502 the Kaisheim altarpiece (Munich), in 1504 the " Basilica of St. Paul," and in 1512 the St. Catherine altarpiece (Augsburg). We know, from sketches and documentary evidence, that the number of commissions actually executed by him must have been far greater. In order to deal with all the orders, a big workshop organisation must have been needed. Holbein's brother Sigmund, and Leonard Beck, an artist with a reputation of his own, were called in as assistants. Then suddenly there came a pause in the production, perhaps produced by economic difficulties. Very few masterpieces were produced between the second decade of the 16th century and Holbein's death in 1524—a few portraits, and the St. Sebastian altarpiece of 1516 (Munich). His last great work, the " Fountain of Life " (Lisbon), was painted far from Augsburg. He had left that town in 1517 and ended his days at Isenheim, where, in the Antonite Church, Grünewald's mighty altarpiece then stood.

The picture that we gain of Holbein's activities as a painter is enhanced by the extensive number of his drawings, which may be divided into two main groups: drawings in pen and wash, closely connected with the paintings, and sketchbooks drawn in silverpoint technique filled chiefly with portraits of his contemporaries. This surviving material is distributed to-day chiefly among the museums of Basle, Berlin, Copenhagen and Bamberg; a single undivided notebook is preserved in the Print Room at Basle.

Holbein's sketches for altarpieces are in marked contrast to the portrait-drawings. Altars, like church interiors, are designed according to the laws of architecture. The church-painter, therefore, made use of the same tools as the architect—compasses, ruler and set-square. The figure subjects were composed by Holbein in constructed space. Like marionettes on a stage, the types he invented appear again recognisably in all the pictures of a series. He perfected this method in the works belonging to the turn of the century, sometimes in powerful groups of figures in violent move- ment, sometimes in quiet, calm arrangements of people, according to the subjects of Holy Scripture. Sketches are known for many of the existing pictures. They are nearly all executed in the same technique. Holbein defines the contours with the pen and washes in the shadow with the brush and Indian ink (Plate 1). Occasionally he begins with a darkly-toned surface on which he draws the composition with the pen, working up the plastic effect of space and figures only by means of black ink and gleaming white (Plate 4).

Anyone who studies Holbein's altarpieces attentively will observe the fact that individuals are painted as well as types, that among the Bible figures are contemporaries of the artist. This shows the way to the sketch-books of the elder Holbein, to the revelations of his personality. In these small volumes, drawn in silverpoint on grey prepared paper, he has left us a vast collection of portraits of the men with whom he came into contact in Augsburg and on his travels (Plates 2, 7, 8, 9, 12-15). We possess no such picture chronicle from the hand of any other German artist. Holbein is keenly interested in each personality that he portrays. He characterises without reserve the rich merchant, the clever monk, the prosperous citizen's wife, the Emperor Maximilian I and his trusted servant and " merry counsellor," Kunz von der Rosen, his friends, finally his brother, his children, and even himself (Plates 2 and 3).

Holbein's style derives from the portrait art of the great Netherlandish artists of the school of Van Eyck. It is unpretentious, without ornamental linear charm, untouched by the far-reaching influence of Dürer. Holbein starts with the contour, the shadows are evolved by means of thicker or more open parallel strokes. Cross-hatching occurs less often. Therefore he was fond of reworking his silverpoint portraits with red chalk on the cheeks and mouths, of emphasising fine shading by drawing with the pen or with the pointed brush and adding high lights in white (for example, Plates 8 and 13).

Holbein introduced portraits from his sketch-books for the first time in the panels of the Frankfort Dominican Altar (Plate 7); the latest known studies of this sort belong to the St. Sebastian Altar of 1516 (Plates 3 and 14). Apart from the many heads, the sketch-books exhibit a number of other interesting documents—workshop accounts, undeciphered notes, studies of the nude and of hands for the pictures (Plate 11), armorial shields, animals and objects of all kinds (Plate 10); then copies after Roman excavations, a Renaissance medal, drawings of classical capitals and ornaments.

Already in early youth, about 1513-14, Holbein's sons, Ambrosius and Hans, left home and started on their travels, by way of Constance to Basle, to study and to seek their fortune in this town of flourishing culture. Owing to the straitened circumstances of the elder Holbein, they could hardly have taken with them any material comforts. We do not know what property they may have inherited from their mother; even her name is unknown to us. But in their father's workshop the sons had seen great altarpieces produced; they would have been called upon to do much of the work. They had also seen how Hans Burgkmair painted side by side with their father, and inspired him to see and to work in the new Italian spirit.

The Master of the two youths at Basle was Hans Herbster. We are unable to judge of this man's artistic qualifications. We know only the portrait that Ambrosius painted of him in 1516 (Basle).

From the surviving œuvre of *Ambrosius Holbein*—as far as one can speak of an œuvre of anyone who died so young—we can only guess at his importance as an artist. By 1515 he was well established at Basle; in 1517 he became a member of the painter's guild and soon afterwards a citizen. With the year 1521 all records disappear. The few small panels painted by Ambrosius—with the exception of a masterpiece at Leningrad—are all to be seen together in the Museum at Basle. An early Madonna picture, still of the Constance period (1514), then a timidly painted " Man of Sorrows," two charming portraits of boys (1518), are almost all that has been preserved, and it is probable that the young artist did not paint much more.

A similar situation exists with regard to the drawings. Scarcely a dozen have survived : Ambrosius sketched a little child in silverpoint and in the same almost timid technique the studies for the painted diptych with the portraits of two boys (Plate 16). His first portrait is the head of a youth with the artist's monogram and the date 1517 (Plate 17). The preparatory drawing in metalpoint is almost entirely concealed by the washes of colour and accents in red chalk. Artistically and technically these drawings are very closely connected with the style of the elder Holbein. Yet Ambrosius lacks that sureness of vision possessed by his father and which is discernible in his brother's earliest works. But he captivates the spectator with the sweetness of his gentle, lyrical style.

Besides the portraits in silverpoint, some pen drawings have been preserved, two roundels with mythological subjects (Plate 18), the design for the sheath of a dagger (Basle) and the " Children's Tournament " (Plate 20). The composition of these drawings, probably designs for goldsmiths, is clear and transparent, sure and full of imaginative invention, like the artist's few woodcuts.

On the spiritual independence and self-assurance of his brother, the still youthfully tentative works of Ambrosius could have no decisive influence.

The course of the human as well as of the artistic career of *Hans Holbein the Younger* was essentially determined by the artist's repeated changes of residence, combined with the most diverse gifts. Between 1514 and 1519 the painter worked at Basle and at Lucerne. To this period belongs the first commission for a portrait, that of the double portrait of the Burgomaster Meyer and his wife. At an early date, Holbein shows himself to have been universally gifted. At Lucerne he decorated the façade and the rooms in the interior of the house of the Mayor, Jakob Hertenstein, with wallpaintings. From Lucerne he wandered to North Italy, probably to Como and Milan. There are no records of such a journey, but ample evidence is to be found in the artist's work. Eagerly he absorbed all impressions : the rich treasure of ornament on the Porta della Rana of Como Cathedral; new solutions of the problems of composition and painting, such as he met with at Milan in the work of Bramante, Leonardo and his pupils. The assimilation of foreign artistic achievements was so complete that he can seldom be accused of plagiarism.

In the following years, between 1519 and 1526, Holbein resided chiefly at Basle. Commissions on a monumental scale—the painting of the façade of the " Haus zum Tanz," frescoes for the Town Hall—were executed. The foundations were laid for his first connexions with the publishers Amerbach and Frobenius. A fruitful era of activity for glass-painting was inaugurated. He painted altarpieces for churches—the altarpiece with scenes from the Passion for the Basle Town Councillor, Hans Oberried (Freiburg i. B.), the " Madonna of Solothurn " for the Getter family (Solothurn).

On a journey to the South of France in 1524, Holbein learnt the technique of the Clouets who made use of coloured chalks in their portrait studies. At Lyons he received commissions from the publishers Melchior and Gaspar Trechsel. The woodcuts of the Dance of Death and those for the Bible were produced for their printing-house. The monuments of Burgundian architecture with their Renaissance ornament stimulated anew his imagination. On his return from France in 1525, Holbein painted for the Burgomaster Meyer his most important Madonna picture (Darmstadt).

On account of the new tendencies of the Reformation, often antagonistic to art, Holbein soon found too little scope at Basle for his artistic activities. In about 1524 he had become acquainted with the great humanist, Erasmus of Rotterdam, whose portrait he painted several times, an acquaintance which was to be of great import-ance to his career. To him Holbein owed his introduction to England, where the art-loving Chancellor, Sir Thomas More, welcomed him into the circle of his closest friends. This was to be the atmosphere most congenial to Holbein's art as a portrait-painter. Single portraits of important English personalities and the large portrait group with many figures which he painted of the Chancellor and his family were the outcome of this happy period of creative activity.

For a few years, between 1528 and 1531, Holbein was again at Basle. During this time he painted the touching portrait of his wife with their two children (Basle) and completed the last three frescoes for the Town Hall.

From 1532 onwards Holbein settled permanently in England. After Sir Thomas More had fallen into disgrace, the German Merchants in London became his chief patrons. He painted the portraits of the rich merchants and decorated their Guildhall with wall-paintings. Eventually, in the middle of the thirties, a connexion was established with Henry VIII, who from 1538 onwards entirely monopolised Holbein as his Court painter. His inexhaustible powers revealed themselves most clearly in the series of the King, his several Queens, and members of the Court, in decorations and wall-paintings for the Palace of Whitehall, in architectural designs and innumer-able sketches for goldsmith's work. In 1543, at the height of his creative activity, the artist was cut off by death. Probably he died of the plague which was then raging in London.

Hans Holbein the Younger is the most prolific of the great masters of the German Renaissance. In addition to the quite exceptional powers of production which he inherited from his father, he achieved extraordinary freedom and facility of method. It is the drawings that most clearly help us understand the full range of Holbein's creative powers. Of many works which have perished, and especially the great monumental paintings, studies and sketches are our only record. One wonders what was the effect of those painted façades, of the Hertensteinhaus, the " Haus zum Tanz," the House with the Emperor enthroned (Plate 35). Probably they were more like gigantic theatrical scenes than clearly designed architecture. Holbein's wall-paintings are not to be interpreted in terms of architecture. They must have appeared both novel and strange in the street setting of a late-Gothic Northern town.

The wall-paintings produced by Holbein for interior decoration appear in a more reassuring light (Plate 34). They too have been preserved only in isolated sketches and copies (the frescoes of the Basle Town Hall, paintings for Whitehall, and the Hall of the Hanse Merchants in the Steelyard in London). The empty stage-setting of the façade paintings disappears. In the decoration of these great rooms, conveying in an easily comprehensible manner the illusion of depth in space, it is the figure element, and the idea that it contains, that is of predominant importance.

Of the drawings which have been preserved, by far the greatest number are por-traits. They are nearly all studies done with a view to painting. The earliest portraits, carefully executed studies in silverpoint for the double portrait of Jakob Meyer and his wife (Plate 22), still recall the keenly observed studies of the elder Holbein's sketch-books. Hans Holbein the Younger drew both of them again ten years later in coloured chalks (Basle) for the big altarpiece which the Burgomaster commissioned him to paint. All youthful timidity is laid aside. It is no longer a matter of the ornamental beauty of individual lines but of the general expression which is concentrated in the features.

Different again are the portraits of the late period. As Courtpainter to Henry VIII, the Master had to exert his powers to the utmost. Commissions for portraits became so plentiful that he could scarcely cope with them all. The famous series of portrait studies at Windsor gives us the clue to Holbein's new method of working. Certainly the treatment these drawings have received in the course of time—their reduction to a standard size, reworking and additions by later owners—has contributed a good deal to the impression of uniformity they make to-day. It has also been suggested that Holbein made use of an apparatus with a glass panel, such as was recommended by Dürer and Leonardo, by means of which he could trace the chief contours from life quickly and surely. It goes against our conception of the creative powers of a supreme master that his imagination should have needed such crutches as these. Yet it is the sign of genius, on the other hand—one has only to think of Dürer's attempts to work out the ideal proportions of the human form by means of mathematical construction—that the creative faculty should employ mechanical methods and rise superior to them. However this may be, the late portrait drawings of Holbein exhibit a consistent, well-considered technique. He lays in the features with coloured chalks and then draws the shadows. To emphasise more important forms, the Master frequently has recourse to the pen. Thus he achieves firm contours in the face, the sharp definition of a coif, the folds of a collar, the down of a fur. Here and there we read abbreviated notes of colour in Holbein's hand. On such a foundation was built the painting for which the portrait drawing served as a model.

The series of portraits of the English Court (Plates 36, 44, 45, 48, 49) invite a comparison with the silverpoint drawings of the elder Holbein. Two worlds are contrasted. The personalities recorded for us by the father are the last witnesses of the dying Middle Ages. The younger Holbein depicts for us the new generation, men of the Renaissance, who have broken the bonds of spiritual subjection.

The severe self-discipline which the younger Holbein imposes on himself in his portraits finds relief in the ornamental fantasy of his designs for applied arts. In the early period they are designs for glass-painters. The various forms of armorial glass created by Holbein remained the models for the whole of the 16th century in Switzerland. In richly decorated Renaissance archways, the artist introduces figures in elaborate *contrapposto* (Plates 24, 28), and fills the intervening space with plants, or clouds, or the view of a landscape. In his technique—pen, brush and Indian ink wash—Holbein reverts to the Augsburg style of draughtsmanship as it was used not only in the altarpiece designs of his father but also in the drawings of Burgkmair.

In the case of the early designs for glass, the imagination is still confined within fixed limits; they are exact models for the glass-painter, drawn pictures. Full creative freedom blossoms forth only in the designs for goldsmith's work of Holbein's latest period. A handle or the sheath of a dagger (Plate 38) forms the framework which Holbein fills with the play of his pen. Human figures and branch-work combine

VII

in a living, neverresting rhythmic curve.   Very often the Master is not satisfied with one study, but draws the same motive several times, always with a different movement (Plate 52).

Drawings which have to be considered as independent, complete works of art in themselves only occupy a small place in Holbein's whole production.   A few of the most beautiful portraits and studies for costume belong to this category (Frontispiece, Plate 46), two watercolours of animals, a bat and a drawing of lambs (Plate 40), also some religious subjects in monochrome technique of the early period (Plates 21 and 26).

To be, like Dürer, a devoted student of landscape and plant life, lay far from Holbein's spiritual disposition.   When he introduces such motives into his pictures, it is with a purely decorative purpose.

The surviving drawings of Hans Holbein the Younger are about 470 in number. Of the German artists of the 16th century, only Dürer has left a greater number; and he has left about twice as many.   Those who wish to see original drawings by Holbein will find good examples in most of the public collections.   But the greatest quantity of his work is preserved in three places: in the Basle Print Room, in the British Museum, and in the Royal Library at Windsor.

In the public collection at Basle there is the half-length portrait of a young man in a rich costume with a red hat.   Ever since the 16th century this drawing has been supposed to be Holbein's self-portrait.   In spite of its no longer perfect condition, it yields a valuable insight into the character of the artist.   We have before us the fine, one might almost say beautiful, features of a young man of about twenty-five.   The clear look in the eyes affords a certain contrast to the soft forms of the features and mouth.   From the dress and the expression one would say he was a man of the world, who seeks the fullness of life not by force but by intelligence.

When Hans Holbein the Younger died in 1543 at the age of 46, the spiritual world recognised, as it has recognised ever since, that he was one of the greatest figures of all times, an " Apelles " of the North, an opinion which remains unchanged to-day. As in Goethe, so in Holbein are united all the gifts of fortune that genius could bring to fruition: an inexhaustible imagination, a never-failing creative faculty, the will to succeed, and a circle of friends to advocate and to further his ideas.   Hans Holbein the Elder was known only in the narrow circle of his German home, a meditative nature, more in touch with the late-Gothic tradition than with the new and mighty currents of the Renaissance.   It remained for the present generation to recognise the importance of the father beside the overwhelming apparition of Hans Holbein the Younger, the father who, as a portrayer of character, was the equal of the son.

NOTES ON THE ILLUSTRATIONS

HANS HOLBEIN THE YOUNGER

Born at Augsburg 1497, died in London 1543.
Painter and designer for woodcut and applied art.

Frontispiece   *Theophraſtus Paracelsus (?)*

Coloured chalks, 401 : 366 mm. Basle, Öffentliche Kunſtsammlung.

The face ſtands out againſt the black surface of the hat, which is used to enclose the composition and to throw the head into relief. The charaċter of the features is suggeſted simply by a few strokes in black chalk and a moſt sparing use of colour, yellow ochre and red.

The drawing dates from shortly before Holbein's firſt journey to England. It is a matter for regret that there is no inscription to identify the arreſting and important personality here portrayed. It has been recently suggeſted that it is a portrait of Theophraſtus of Hohenheim, the doċtor, called Paracelsus; and this hypothesis is supported, in the firſt place by his resemblance to authentic likenesses of the celebrated scholar, and in the second by the faċt that in the summer of 1526 Paracelsus ſtayed at Basle in the house of Holbein's publisher, Frobenius.

HANS HOLBEIN THE ELDER

Born at Augsburg about 1460-70, died at Isenheim in 1524. Painter and designer for woodcut and glass-painting.

I   *The Virgin as Queen of Heaven*

Pen, brush and wash, 205 : 191 mm. Weimar, Schlossmuseum.

This drawing is of the Maſter's early period, before 1500. Holbein has carried out the composition in the utmoſt detail. The Virgin sits on a large cushion, wearing the Crown of Heaven, and presents her Child to the faithful. Two angels hold the sceptre and orb, the insignia of majesty, and support the train of her mantle. The Child plays with a rope of pearls, and takes no notice of the apple which his mother offers Him.

2a   *Ambrosius and Hans Holbein*

The inscription in the artiſt's hand reads : 1511 prosy Holbein 14 Hanns.
Silverpoint, 103 : 155 mm. Berlin, Kupferſtichkabinett.

It is only natural that a portrait-painter should make frequent use of his family as models. The earlieſt portraits of Ambrosius and Hans Holbein occur in the piċture of the " Basilica of St. Paul " (Augsburg Gallery), where the two children appear ſtanding beside their father in the lower corner of the composition. They were then—about 1504—ten and seven years old respeċtively; in the present drawing of 1511 they are seventeen and fourteen.

2b

Sigmund Holbein

Dated 1512. Silverpoint, 130 : 96 mm. London, British Museum.

The inscription, which originally read simply " Sigmund Holbein maler " (Sigmund Holbein the painter), has been amplified by a later hand with the words " Hans pruder des alten " (brother of the elder Hans). An exactly similar profile portrait is in the Berlin Printroom. It may be supposed that Holbein occasionally copied his own drawings, perhaps because they were particularly successful.

Sigmund was by nature no more than a studio-assistant. We know that in 1501 he was helping his brother at Frankfort; and about 1517 he had a case at law against his employer. He, too, like his nephews, was forced to wander westward; he died in Berne in 1540. No certainly authentic works of his are known.

3

Self-portrait

Inscribed " Hanns Holbein, maler Der alt " (Hans Holbein, painter, the elder) and " Da ich w..."
Silverpoint, touched with red and white, 130 : 100 mm. Chantilly, Musée Condé.

It was an old custom among artists, in the great panel-pictures that they painted for the Church, to perpetuate their own features in some humble position among the choir of the Saints.

In Holbein's St. Sebastian altar in the Munich Gallery, on the outer wing with St. Elizabeth of Hungary, appears the bearded head of the artist himself, looking up at the Saint from the lower corner, behind a disease-stricken beggar. This is the study for that self-portrait.

4

The Death of the Virgin

Dated 1508. Pen, brush and wash on reddish brown paper, heightened with white,
300 : 192 mm. Basle, Öffentliche Kunstsammlung.

Original studies by the Master for numerous panel-pictures have survived. They are done on different principles to the drawings in his sketch-books (see Introduction, p. III). The present sheet is the design for the wing of an altarpiece; but we know nothing of its eventual execution. The scene is laid in a Romanesque church-interior. Usually the dying Virgin is represented with all the apostles around her. Holbein gives a simplified version of the event. St. John is handing her the candle; and there are only one woman, reading prayers, and two apostles standing in the background. Above, the soul of the Virgin is flying off to Heaven in the form of a maiden in prayer (cf. also note to Plate 9).

5

St. George Slaying the Dragon

Pen, brush and wash, 206 : 310 mm. Basle, Öffentliche Kunstsammlung.

There are not many compositions among Holbein's works as elaborately decorative as this. A serious subject is transformed into a playful fantasy, in the true late-Gothic spirit. The drawing is one of a series of Saints, all of the same size and enclosed in a border-line, with a large Roman H as signature below. They were probably designs for glass-painting.

6

Head of an Old Man

Silverpoint, 111 : 103 mm. Copenhagen, Printroom.

Holbein's art takes a new direction about the turn of the century, as the altarpiece of 1500-1501, painted for the Dominicans of Frankfort, reveals. In the scenes from the Passion, particularly, the artist displays, at this moment in his career, dramatic forms of expression such as he never attempted in his later work. Possibly here his path crossed that of Grünewald, the greatest painter of his time.

The old man here depicted, opening his mouth in a malicious laugh, is reminiscent of the tormentors of Christ in the Frankfort Passion-subjects. May this not be a self-portrait? Is it possible that Holbein made studies in facial expression before his mirror, as the young Rembrandt did?

7 *Johann von Wilnau, Prior of the Dominican Monastery at Frankfort (d. 1516)*

Silverpoint, 137 : 90 mm. Bamberg, Staatsbibliothek.

This portrait is a record of the features of an extraordinary person. Johann von Wilnau was of equal importance as preacher and organiser, as teacher, builder and patron of the arts. It was thanks to him that the Dominican Church at Frankfort was decorated with a unique series of paintings; it was he who called upon the greatest masters of the period, Holbein, Dürer and Grünewald, Hans Baldung Grien and the Hausbuch Master, to paint altarpieces for the interior.

This drawing served as a study for the head of St. Dominic in the genealogical tree of the Dominican order on the High Altar.

8 *Girl with long flowing Hair*

Silverpoint, pen and black ink, heightened with white, 154 : 102 mm.
Paris, École des Beaux-Arts (Masson Collection).

The portrait of this little girl, plain as she is, is most sympathetically drawn. The tone of the silverpoint, which yields but little contrast, is here not sufficient for the artist's needs; he adds the shadows under the waves of the hair with the pen, and gives them a delicate sheen by means of high-lights in white.

9 *Portrait of a Boy*

Silverpoint, red chalk, brush and wash, 133 : 83 mm. Basle, Öffentliche Kunstsammlung.

The boy must have been a favourite model of his master. He appears again as St. John in the Study for the wing of an altarpiece with the Death of the Virgin (Plate 4). It has been supposed that this clean-cut little head is a portrait of the painter's eldest son Ambrosius, who was fourteen years old when the study for the altarpiece, which is dated 1508, was done. This hypothesis has much in its favour; for the intelligent-looking boy in the present drawing might be about that age.

10 *Sheet of Studies with two miniature Violins and a Cock*

Silverpoint on grey ground, 107 : 155 mm. Basle, Öffentliche Kunstsammlung.

The artist must always have carried a sketchbook about with him in his pocket, and thus was able to seize upon everything that caught his eye. Objects that have no connexion with one another, such as the cock and the musical instruments here, are noted side by side. Scattered about among these artistic notes are often to be found calculations of income and expenditure, or jottings about the events of the day, written with the same metal point.

The musical instrument here depicted is a rebeck. This form of small violin often occurs in the work of the Venetian painters of the 15th and 16th centuries—Carpaccio, Giovanni Bellini and Cima da Conegliano. In the " Coronation of the Virgin " by Baldung in Freiburg Cathedral, there is a little angel playing on a similar instrument.

11   *Studies of Hands*

Silverpoint on grey ground, 140 : 100 mm. Basle, Öffentliche Kunstsammlung.

This is a sheet of studies from nature, intended for use in pictures. Holbein made use of them particularly in the Kaisheim altarpiece of 1502 (Munich, Alte Pinakothek); certain of the motives in the drawing can be clearly recognized in the hands of the executioners, holding the instruments of the Passion.

12   *The writing-master Leonhard Wagner*

Silverpoint, 140 : 104 mm. Copenhagen, Printroom.

Holbein here gives us the portrait of the writing-master Leonhard Wirstlin, called Wagner, of Schwabmünchen near Augsburg. The inscription on the sheet—" Herr Lienhart [Leonhard] has invented 115 different sorts of writing "—draws attention to the profession of the sitter, who was to play an important part in the development of German lettering. It may be assumed that he was the inventor of the Gothic " Maximilian " type that was used for the Emperor in the Prayer Book of 1512 and in the " Theuerdank " of 1517. Wagner died in 1522 in Augsburg, at the Monastery of SS. Ulrich and Afra, aged 68. The features of the learned monk are recorded for us in two other silverpoint drawings by the Master.

13   *Ulrich Artzt, Burgomaster of Augsburg*

Silverpoint, brush and wash, 139 : 102 mm. Copenhagen, Printroom.

The inscription—Ulrich Artzet, Burgomaster and Captain of the Confederacy—refers to the appointment of Artzt as Captain of the Suabian Confederacy of 1511. The artist takes special pleasure in the rendering of the hair and the fur. By means of strong pen work, over the delicate lines of the metal-point, he achieves a very naturalistic effect. There are two further portraits of this important personage in the Berlin and Bamberg Printrooms

14   *A Crossbowman*

Silverpoint and brush, heightened with white, on grey ground, 119 : 95 mm.
Copenhagen, Printroom.

In the year 1516 Holbein the elder finished the St. Sebastian altarpiece for the Nunnery of St. Catherine at Augsburg, a masterpiece of his late period, which in its composition betrays the influence of the Renaissance. The various panels belonging to it are now in the Munich Gallery; and besides the self-portrait of the artist (Plate 3), a number of other separate studies have survived. In the motive of the crossbowman taking aim, an essential change takes place between the first sketch and the final execution : in the silverpoint drawing he is simply a crossbowman; in the picture he becomes one of the cruel executioners of the Saint.

15   *"A jolly good fellow "*

Silverpoint, pen and red chalk, heightened with white, 106 : 140 mm.
Basle, Öffentliche Kunstsammlung.

Only five words are legible of a longer inscription, which probably contained also the young man's name. But what is legible yields a welcome explanation of the subject. The word *"Gesell"* was used in those days not only for a painter's assistant, but also his friend. Dedications of the 16th century often end with the words : " *zum guten Gedächtnis meinem lieben Gesellen* " (a souvenir for a dear good fellow).

AMBROSIUS HOLBEIN

Born 1494 at Augsburg, died probably after 1521 at Basle. Painter and designer for woodcut.

16   *Portrait of a Boy*

Silverpoint, 141 : 102 mm. Basle, Öffentliche Kunstsammlung.

In the Basle Picture Gallery are two painted portraits of children by Ambrosius Holbein. They are established as authentic works of his hand in the 16th century inventory of the Amerbach Collection, which forms the nucleus of the Basle collection of drawings: " *item zwei Kneblin in gelben Kleidern uf holtz mit Ölfarben Ambrosi Holbein* " (Item, two little boys in yellow dress, in oil colours on wood, Ambrosi Holbein). By a stroke of good fortune, both the preliminary drawings for these portraits have survived, the one here reproduced in Basle, the other in the Albertina at Vienna. They are not rapid sketches from the life, but carefully finished portrait studies. It is particularly pleasant to be able to compare the studies with the paintings, and to see how in certain small details the artist has tried to improve upon his own idea, while in other places he has followed the study exactly. On the whole we are inclined to prefer the first idea, since it gives a more immediate impression of the living model.

17   *Portrait of a Youth*

Signed with the monogram A H and dated 1517. Red chalk and brush with black and brown wash, over metal-point, 202 : 154 mm. Basle, Öffentliche Kunstsammlung.

Ambrosius himself must have considered this one of his best works. He employs a noticeably mixed technique. The preliminary drawing in metal-point is almost completely obscured by strokes of red chalk in the flesh and brownish black shadows both in face and hair. The cap and the eyebrows are in still darker colours.

18   *Pyramus and Thisbe at the Well*

Signed A H and dated 1518. Pen, diameter 65 mm. Carlsruhe, Kunsthalle.

There is a companion piece to this little drawing, also at Carlsruhe, with Hercules throttling Antaeus. Holbein has modified the real character of the scenes depicted; two themes of a naturally tragic order acquire in his conception a graceful and charming liveliness.

The compositions are rather crowded, and not well adapted to the circular shape. The linework is so clearly executed with the pen, that both drawings have the appearance of early etchings. They were undoubtedly intended to be carried out in some such technique, for decorative purposes. The story of the unhappy lovers Pyramus and Thisbe was known to Holbein from Ovid, Metamorphoses, IV, 4—415.

HANS HOLBEIN THE YOUNGER

Born at Augsburg 1497, died in London 1543. Painter and designer for woodcut
and applied art.

19   *Penelope at her Loom*

Pen. The detail reproduced is the size of the original. Basle, Öffentliche Kunstsammlung.

In the year 1515 Frobenius of Basle published the first edition of the celebrated " *Lob der Narrheit* " (Praise of Folly) by Erasmus of Rotterdam. In a copy that belonged to the schoolmaster Oswald Mycenius of Lucerne, to whom Holbein owed his introduction to the ideas of the Humanists, the artist executed as border-decorations, within the space of a few days, his earliest illustrations. The 81 pen drawings that the book contains are not all of equal importance; but they bear witness to the young artist's humour and wealth of imagination, and to the rapidity of his artistic development. In the passage here illustrated by Holbein, Erasmus writes, that if one tried to combat the arguments of Scholasticism, "the same thing would happen as on Penelope's loom in the story."

AMBROSIUS HOLBEIN

Born 1494 at Augsburg, died probably after 1521 at Basle. Painter and designer for woodcut.

20 *Tournament of Children*

Pen, 262 : 74 mm. Berlin, Staatliche Kunstbibliothek.

The decorative filling of the space, with branchwork and figure motives intertwined, is reminiscent of the ever-restless rhythm of late-Gothic forms, such as we find for instance in the work of Israel van Meckenem, the engraver of the lower Rhine district. It is in marked contrast to the clear, orderly conception of the younger Hans Holbein, who constructs his compositions in the spirit of the Renaissance.

It may be supposed that the drawing was intended as a model for etching on metal, like the design for a dagger-sheath, which is at Basle.

HANS HOLBEIN THE YOUNGER

Born at Augsburg 1497, died in London 1543. Painter and designer for woodcut
and applied art.

21 *The Man of Sorrows seated on the Cross*

Dated 1519. Pen, brush and wash on brown ground, heightened with white. 157 : 205 mm.
Berlin, Kupferstichkabinett.

The artist achieves with his chiaroscuro technique a twofold effect, purely pictorial and at the same time evocative of sentiment. Like Altdorfer in his "Blue Night in the Wood," so Holbein with the deep brown of his Passion scenes awakens in the spectator serious and solemn feelings. At the same time, a pictorial value is created by the preparatory grounding of the paper which produces an effect of polychrome by the simplest means—dark ink and heightening with white.

According to the date (1519), this drawing was done during Holbein's stay at Lucerne or in the first weeks after his return to Basle. This early work exemplifies the Baroque tendencies of late-Gothic art in the Upper Rhine district, which temporarily made a deep impression on the young Holbein.

22 *Jakob Meyer, Burgomaster of Basle*

Silverpoint and red chalk on prepared paper. 281 : 191 mm.
Basle, Öffentliche Kunstsammlung.

This important portrait study was drawn directly from life. In order to strengthen his own impression, the Master adds short notes of colour to the drawing: "ar-ogen schwarz-baret rot-mosfarb-brauenn gelber dan das har-grusenn wit brauenn" (eyes black-cap red-green-brows more yellow than the hair-curly hair like the brows). At the same time as this drawing of the Burgomaster, in the year 1516, Holbein drew his second wife, Dorothea Kannengiesser. Both sketches were used as studies for the double portrait, now in the Basle Gallery. In 1516 Jakob Meyer zum Hasen was Burgomaster at the age of about 34. He was one of Holbein's most important patrons. Shortly before Holbein's first journey to England (1525-26), he commissioned him to paint the famous Madonna (Darmstadt, Schloss) in which he appears as donor with his family.

23   *The Virgin and St. John beside the Cross*

With the monogram H. H. Pen and wash, heightened with white and red, 210 : 156 mm.
Augsburg, Maximiliansmuseum.

This is one of the Master's earliest works. The technique and form of expression are closely related to the style of the elder Holbein. In spite of that, the composition is new and daring. The Crucifix is placed in a commanding position at an angle to the picture-plane. The figures of St. John and the Virgin are raised as though on a platform. The scene is probably intended to suggest the words of Christ, spoken from the Cross to the Virgin : " Woman, behold thy Son !" and to St. John: " Behold thy Mother !" (John XIX, 26, 27).

24   *Design for Glass with the arms of Hans Fleckenstein*

Pen, brush and wash, about 419 : 285 mm. Brunswick, Herzog Anton Ulrich-Museum.

On the tablet beneath the coat of arms is the inscription: "Hans Fleckenstein" and the date 1517. The signature " J. Holbain " has been added by a later owner. A scribbled word or two, scarcely legible to us, record the colouring. St. Barbara and St. Sebastian who appear on the cornice over the shield-bearers were the patron saints of Hans Fleckenstein, a citizen of Lucerne.

25   *Leaina before the Judges*

Pen, brush and wash, 180 : 137 mm. Basle, Öffentliche Kunstsammlung.

In the year 1517 Holbein was commissioned by the Mayor of Lucerne to decorate his house with wall-paintings. The Renaissance palaces of North Italy served as the painter's model.
The episode of Leaina before the judges is taken from ancient history. The mistress of Aristogeiton bit her tongue off in order not to have to betray the tyrant's murderer. The sketch belongs to the series of five pictures that adorned the top floor under the roof; the companion picture represented the death of Lucretia. To suit the viewpoint of the spectator on the ground, the great hall in which the scene takes place is represented in sharp perspective; the disturbing white spaces in the composition show where the rafters rest against the wall.

26   *St. Adrian*

Pen, brush and wash on grey prepared paper, heightened with white, 277 : 180 mm.
Paris, Louvre.

In about 300 A. D. St. Adrian was a Roman officer under Galerius Maximianus; he was converted to Christianity and died a martyr. He is venerated by the faithful as the patron saint of soldiers and mercenaries and as the patron of smiths (note the anvil). Since the end of the 14th century, he has also been invoked as one of the protectors against plague.
From the grisaille technique and the style of the composition, we may conclude that we have here the model for the wing of an altarpiece. Yet nothing is known of this work.
St. Adrian is not to be found among Swiss saints; he is known chiefly in the west of Europe. Perhaps the drawing has some connexion with Holbein's journey to France in the year 1524.

27   *The Madonna in the Niche*

Pen, brush and wash, 208 : 155 mm. Brunswick, Herzog Anton Ulrich-Museum.

This design is dated 1520 and bears the Master's monogram. The drawing was the property of the well-known glass-painter of Schaffhausen, Daniel Lindtmayer (about 1522 to about 1606). On the back he has written the following appreciative remark: " *Dass ſtücklin iſt dess Daniel Lindtmayer maller von Schaffhausen | ess iſt jm garr lieb.*" (This little piece belongs to Daniel Lindtmayer, painter of Schaffhausen / it is very dear to him.)

The fusion of Southern charm of form and Northern sentiment is moſt happy and makes the drawing particularly attraĉtive.

28   *The Standardbearer of Livinentals*

Pen, brush, with brown wash, 428 : 318 mm. Berlin, Kupferſtichkabinett.

The Landsknecht, who ſtands in the opening of a window, holds in his hand a banner on which appears St. Ambrose, the patron saint of Livinentals. The landscape with the view of the bridlepath over the St. Gothard and the little church is probably the earlieſt view, though it may not be a topographically correĉt one, of this Alpine pass; Holbein probably travelled into Italy this way. The spandrels of the arch are filled by the " Judgment of Paris," intended as a purely decorative motive; it has no bearing on the chief theme of the composition.

29   *St. Kunigunda*

Design for glass. Pen and brush, richly coloured with washes of red, green, brown, and bleu, 316 : 206 mm. Berlin, Kupferſtichkabinett.

The Empress Kunigunda (d. 1039), wife of Henry II, has been venerated as a saint since the 13th century. She was closely connected with Basle; her husband consecrated the new Cathedral in 1019, and the Empress herself presented a coſtly Crucifix with relics of the True Cross. Holbein painted the Saint a second time, holding the Cross, on one of the doors of the organ loft of the Basle Cathedral (Basle, Museum). We are tempted to suppose that this design for glass was intended for a window in the Cathedral too.

30   *Study from the Model for the Madonna of Solothurn*

Silverpoint and red chalk, worked over with the brush, 197 : 165 mm. Paris, Louvre.

In the head of this young girl, the artiſt has probably left us a portrait of his wife. He idealises his model in the Altarpiece of 1522. They are the same features, but more mature and dignified.

Six years later, Holbein painted his wife with their two children (Basle, Öffentliche Kunſtsammlung). There is but little resemblance between this well-eſtablished portrait and the early ſtudy; only great misfortune could have altered anyone so much in so short a time.

The motto on the dress, which was probably embroidered, reads: "Als. In. Ern. Als. In." (Ever in honour.)

31   *Jean de France, Duc de Berry (d. 1416)*

Coloured chalks, 397 : 275 mm. Basle, Öffentliche Kunſtsammlung.

From a letter written by Erasmus of Rotterdam to the Nuremberg humaniſt, Wilibald Pirkheimer, we know that Holbein undertook a journey to France in the year 1524. Two drawings done from the effigies on the tombs of the Duc de Berry and his wife, in the Cathedral at Bourges, bear witness to this journey. These studies are no ordinary sketches from the note-book of a painter on his travels, but magnificent translations of sculptured form.

32 *The Leper*

Dated 1523. Coloured chalks on pink tinted paper, washed with colour and worked over
with the pen, 205 : 150 mm. Cambridge (Mass.). Collection of Alice and Paul J. Sachs.

Holbein depicts with devastating realism the affliction of this young man. We do not often find portraits which embody the traces of a tragic fate in such moving fashion. The miserable expression of the sick man rivets the attention of the spectator. In the Middle Ages leprosy, introduced from the East, was a widely-spread disease; at the gates of cities there were usually leper-houses where the unfortunate sufferers lived.

33 *Woman throwing stones*

Pen, brush and wash on red-brown prepared paper, heightened with white, 204 : 122 mm.
Basle, Öffentliche Kunstsammlung.

The search for the ideal human form was among the fundamental problems of the Renaissance. While one artist constructs laws of proportion on mathematical lines, another aspires to solve the problem in studying from the life. Like Leonardo and Dürer, Holbein attempted ideal constructions. This "Woman throwing stones" is a mature work of the Master's and shows complete mastery of the anatomy of the female form. The figure has the effect of a piece of sculpture. Emphasis is laid not on the athletic exercise, but on the rhythmical grace of the dancing movement.

34 *Rehoboam threatening his father's Councillors and the Elders of the People*

Pen, brush and wash with watercolours, 226 : 380 mm. Basle, Öffentliche Kunstsammlung.

The large wall-paintings which Holbein did at two different periods of his life—1521 and 1530—for the Town Hall at Basle, are only to be reconstructed to-day from a few original fragments, at Basle, Öffentliche Kunstsammlung, and from sketches and copies. The subjects were taken from the Old Testament and from Roman history.

The subject of Rehoboam threatening the Councillors and the Elders of the people was painted in the months of July and November 1530, after Holbein's return from England. The sketch reproduced here dates from the middle of the twenties. The scene illustrates the episode which after Solomon's death led to the division of the Kingdom. The moment chosen for representation is that of Rehoboam's threat: " My father chastised you with whips, but I shall chastise you with scorpions." (I, Kings, 12, Verse 11.) The Councillors are seen turning away in anger; in the landscape background, we see the result of the threat: Jeroboam is there being crowned as a rival king.

The choice of this particular theme for the Town Hall was probably intended to suggest that a government can only stand with the consent of the people.

35 *Design for the façade of a House*

Pen, brush and wash, with a preliminary drawing in black chalk, about 171 : 198 mm.
Basle, Öffentliche Kunstsammlung.

Holbein was always obliged to adapt his façade decorations to an existing scheme of architecture. The wall-surfaces of Gothic houses were not always symmetrically divided by the apertures of windows and doors, and were consequently not very easily adapted to a Renaissance style of decoration.

This study for a house-façade with an Emperor enthroned is only the fragment of a larger design which evidently continued below to a considerable extent. The dominating figure of the monarch is introduced between two windows.

It is probable that the work was commissioned by Bonifazius Amerbach; his house in Basle was called " Das Haus zum Kaiserstuhl " (the House with the Emperor's Throne).

36   *John More, son of the Chancellor Sir Thomas More*

Black chalk and watercolours, 380 : 280 mm. Windsor Castle, Royal Library. (Copyright of His Majesty the King.)

Holbein's most important portrait group, that of the Chancellor Sir Thomas More with his family, was painted in the year 1527. A complete sketch for it is preserved in the Basle Museum. The figure of Henry VIII's noble-minded Chancellor forms the centre of the composition. On his left sits his aged father, John More; on his right stands his nineteen-year-old son, John, reading a book.

Besides the present drawing, there are seven other portrait-studies for the painting in the collection at Windsor; among them the portrait of the Chancellor himself. These drawings give us valuable information about Holbein's method of working and show us how he devoted the most careful study to each individual.

The drawing is inscribed with some notes of colour in Holbein's hand referring to the costume: " lipfarb brun," implying that the sitter's coat was reddish-brown.

37   *Portrait of an unknown Lady*

Coloured chalks, 402 : 290 mm. Windsor Castle, Royal Library. (Copyright of His Majesty the King.)

Holbein evidently sketched this portrait with great rapidity in broad chalk strokes. Only a little red enlivens the yellow flesh tones. Written notes, such as: " atless " (satin), " dam " (damask), " rot " (red) take the place of colouring. The drawing conveys the effect of a momentary impression. We do not know the name of the lady, but her type and her dress tell us something definite about her origin; she is certainly Flemish. She reminds us of the portraits of Gerard David of the beginning of the 16th century (e. g. the silverpoint Study of a Girl with Violets in the Louvre).

38   *Design for the Sheath of a Swiss Dagger*

About 1528-31. Pen drawing, 282 : 69 mm. Basle, Öffentliche Kunstsammlung.

Holbein was set other tasks than those of the ordinary painter and draughtsman. The Master delighted in adapting his art to the needs of the craftsman. Nevertheless the goldsmith who aspired to follow faithfully with his chisel the artist's playful penmanship in these antique scenes would not find his task an easy one. So the surviving works executed after Holbein's designs do in fact appear coarse in comparison with the original sketches. This dagger sheath was intended for a purely ornamental weapon, not an object of practical use. Scenes from mythology were familiar to the fashionable world of the day. In three compartments arranged one above the other appear Venus and Cupid, Thisbe with the dead Pyramus and the judgment of Paris.

39 *Parnassus*

Pen drawing, brush and wash with watercolours, 521 : 384 mm. Berlin, Kupferstichkabinett.

This elaborate design represents a festive decoration arranged by Holbein for the Coronation procession of Queen Anne Boleyn on May 31, 1533. The decoration adorned the Steelyard, the Guildhouse of the German merchants in London. According to contemporary descriptions, it is to be supposed that it was not actually a painting, but rather a *tableau vivant* arranged before a painted scene. In an airy arbour, surmounted by an imperial eagle of state, sits Apollo, surrounded by singing Muses. The group is flanked by two ornamental columns intended for the arms of the King and Queen. A Renaissance fountain emphasizes the centralized balance of the composition. According to one description of the feast, the fountain flowed with wine which was dispensed to the people all day.

40 *A Lamb and the Head of a Lamb*

Watercolours, 206 : 246 mm. Basle, Öffentliche Kunstsammlung.

Only a very few of Holbein's studies from live animals have survived; a bat, a trout, and a snail are among them. Most of his pictures of animals are derived purely from the imagination; natural appearance is sacrificed for the sake of the ornamental.

These two drawings are sketched entirely with the brush. The colouring of the lambs' coats is indescribably delicate, varying between tones of brown and grey; tender rose colour heightened with white is used for the heads in nose, eyes and ears.

41 *Five Musicians in a Gallery*

Pen, brush and wash, 130 : 182 mm. London, British Museum.

Holbein has observed these five musicians with considerable humour. The three performers on the woodwind instruments are absorbed in their art, while the rounded cheeks of the performers on the tuba and the trumpet are eloquent of the effort required by these instruments.

The drawing is probably a fragment from a bigger design for a wall-painting. It is of the same date as the paintings done for Henry VIII in the Palace of Whitehall, about 1537.

42 *The fair Phyllis*

Pen, brush and wash, 133 : 83 mm. Dessau, Anhaltische Gemäldegalerie.

In this charming sketch, Holbein has depicted one of those fair ladies of the time whose outward appearance evidently fascinated him even if he remained indifferent to their fate. She is the type of the " fair Offenburger," whom he immortalised in two pictures as Lais and Venus. Phyllis, the mistress of Aristotle, is often represented riding on the old man's back and controlling him with the reins. But Holbein may also have intended the woman with the bridle to represent Nemesis, the baneful Goddess of Destiny.

43 *Study of Costume*

Pen, watercolour wash, 230 : 162 mm. London, British Museum.

In order to appreciate this drawing, it is necessary to have an idea of the colours of this simple and broadly defined figure. The light colour of the coat detaches itself from the vivid blue of the mantle; a further colour-contrast is afforded by the reddish-brown of the high leather boots. The elegant gentleman wears wooden clogs on his feet as a protection against cold and wet.

44   *Portrait of an unknown Lady*

Coloured chalks, 355 : 246 mm. Windsor Castle, Royal Library.
(Copyright of His Majesty the King.)

The colour scheme of this drawing is very delicate. The black chalks are broken only by touches of yellow and red in the face; the ground of the paper is not of an even tone. The technique affords essential evidence for dating the portrait; it belongs to the period of Holbein's first visit to England, about 1527-28. The unknown lady used to be thought to be the nurse of Edward VI.

45   *John Fisher, Bishop of Rochester*

Coloured chalks worked over with brush and wash, 381 : 232 mm. Windsor Castle,
Royal Library. (Copyright of His Majesty the King.)

Like his father, Holbein occasionally made several repetitions of one of his portraitdrawings (see the text to Plates 2b, 12, 13), so that it is often hard for us to determine which was the original conception. Often, too, the original was copied by contemporaries. The Windsor Castle portrait of the Bishop of Rochester survives in two later repetitions.

We know that Holbein became acquainted with John Fisher through Erasmus of Rotterdam or Sir Thomas More whose friend he was. The drawing shows him at the age of 59. John Fisher, a powerful opponent of the Reformation, was beheaded in 1535, after opposing Henry VIII's wishes in the matter of divorce, and was canonised together with his fellowmartyr, Sir Thomas More, four hundred years after his death.

46   *Self-portrait of Holbein at the age of about Forty*

Coloured chalks, heightened with white on pink prepared paper, 372 : 304 mm.
Basle, Dr. R. Geigy-Schlumberger Collection.

We know three drawings which can claim to be self-portraits of Holbein. Of these the portrait in coloured chalks of the year 1543, in the Uffizi at Florence, is the most important. The celebrated early self-portrait at the age of about twenty-five at Basle (Öffentliche Kunstsammlung) is mentioned in records of the late 16th century (see Introduction, page VIII). The identification of our portrait, which would belong to the late thirties, is based on the likeness to a miniature (London, Wallace Collection) in which the artist represents himself painting, and to the drawing in Florence.

47   *Portrait of an unknown Man*

Coloured chalks, pen and wash on pink toned paper, 272 : 210 mm. Windsor Castle,
Royal Library. (Copyright of His Majesty the King.)

This drawing with its powerful colour-contrasts and the exquisite rendering of detail is an exception to the series of delicately toned portrait drawings at Windsor Castle. The gentleman's face was laid in with coloured chalks in the usual way; the whole picture was then worked over by the artist's hand in the head and dress with brush and wash, producing a compact and powerful effect. According to the written notes of colour, the nobleman wore a coat of black and red satin.

It is believed that the man portrayed was a Southern Frenchman; probably he was a member of the French Embassy, resident in London in the year 1533.

Coloured chalks on pink prepared ground, drawn over with wash and brush, 305 : 210 mm.
Windsor Castle, Royal Library. (Copyright of His Majesty the King.)

The old inscription on this drawing probably refers to the mother of Sir Anthony Hemingham
or Heveningham of Ketteringham in Norfolk. But it has also been supposed that the lady is
Margaret Roper, the daughter of Sir Thomas More. The portrait cannot belong to the celebrated
family group of 1527, however (see text to Plate 36), for the studies for this picture are executed
in a different technique.

For many of his portraits of women, Holbein employs the same method of draughtsmanship.
The general design is carried out in black chalk; in the head-dress occur ochre, red chalk and brown
tones, and there are in the mouth, cheeks and eyes light accents of red; high lights are added in
white chalk. Finally the artist introduces lines and flat washes of black with the brush, which
hold the whole structure of the portrait together like a scaffolding.

49   *Portrait of an unknown Lady*

Coloured chalks on pink toned paper, pen, 270 : 168 mm. Windsor Castle, Royal Library.
(Copyright of His Majesty the King.)

The features are modelled with great delicacy over the fine tones of rubbed chalk. Holbein draws
firm contours with the pen, strengthens the oval of the head, the eyes, mouth and nose, and indicates
the embroidery on the shirt. The notes : "samet" (velvet) and "damast" (damask) are also from
the artist's hand.

The lady represented is possibly Amalie of Cleves, the sister of the Queen, Anne of Cleves.

50   *Three designs for Orders*

Pen, brush and wash, 63 : 92 and 70 : 70 mm. Basle, Öffentliche Kunstsammlung.

These three sketches are designs for medallions to be worn on a chain round the neck. In-
numerable ornaments like these, mostly of silvergilt, of the 15th and 16th centuries, have survived.

The medallions showing St. Michael fighting the Dragon were probably designed by Holbein
for the Order of St. Michael founded by Louis XI of France. The other medallion was probably
intended as the badge of a brotherhood of St. Roch. An Angel kneels at the feet of the Saint,
tending the sores on his leg. In all parts of Europe in the Middle Ages, brotherhoods were founded for the care of the plague-stricken; St. Roch was their patron saint.

51   *Mirror Frame with Mermaid and Cupids*

Pen drawing, 150 : 106 mm. Basle, Öffentliche Kunstsammlung.

In its ornamental design, the frame is strictly symmetrical in arrangement. The figures, too, are
skilfully introduced into the general rhythm. It is only on a closer inspection that we see that each
putto is treated individually. The crouching mermaid who forms the foot of the frame, and Cupid
with his playfellows, are to be taken as symbols which may have had some connexion with the
origin of the mirror and its fair owner. Only in the work of Dürer do we find penmanship of this
quality, revealing within the limits of the smallest space the inexhaustible imagination of a great
master.

XXI

Design for a Table Ornament

Pen drawing, 262 : 124 mm. Basle, Öffentliche Kunstsammlung.

The artist designs only half of the table ornament; this implies that it is intended to be completely symmetrical. The draughtsman often obtains the complete design by taking an offset of the drawing on a damp sheet of paper, then placing offset and original side by side. This study allows us to follow the process of its production to a quite exceptional degree; for Holbein after completing the design took single details out of the whole composition and drew them again in order to make the form clear. The allegorical figures cannot all be identified. Half-length female figures with wings carrying baskets of fruit on their heads sit on the rim of the large cup; above appears a sacrificial scene, surmounted by Zeus with his thunderbolt.

Design for a covered Goblet

Pen drawing, 350 : 198 mm. Basle, Öffentliche Kunstsammlung.

This design for a goblet is fundamentally different from the designs for goldsmith's work in the " English Sketch-book " (see Plates 50-52, 56) drawn at high speed from the first inspiration. It is a case not of an immediate jotting down of an idea, but of a completed model, intended for the goldsmith's direct use. Besides the simple volutes, Holbein proposes as a foot for the goblet a variation with a ram's head, which he adds as a note to the whole composition.

Edward Prince of Wales, Son of Henry VIII

Pen drawing, 50 mm. in diameter. Basle, Öffentliche Kunstsammlung.

The portrait of the child, based on previous studies, is carefully designed within the circle. Each details receives its irrevocable place in the composition. The goldsmith who was to execute the design in engraving or in enamel was thus given precise lines to follow in his work. The features of the two-year-old Prince have been preserved in a portrait of Holbein's of the year 1538 (Washington, Mellon Collection). We know that Holbein presented King Henry VIII with this portrait of his son as a New Year's gift in 1539. Perhaps the gift inspired the idea of the goldsmith's work, for which Holbein was required to furnish the design.

Tantalus

Pen and watercolour, 53 mm. in diameter. New York, Philip Hofer Collection.

This delicately executed little drawing produces the effect of an enamel. Against the blue sky is placed the apple tree with hanging branches, harmoniously introduced into the curve of the roundel. The branches are heightened with gold. The face of Tantalus, the landscape and the scroll are illuminated with tones of rose, grey, and brown.

Holbein faithfully illustrates the story as it is told in Homer's Odyssey (XI, 582 ss.). Tantalus must do penance for his wanton behaviour to the Gods, by languishing eternally; the fruit and water which surround him shrink away from him whenever he wishes to quench his thirst.

Two Designs for Jewellery, a Pendant and a Brooch

Pen, brush and wash, 66 : 35 mm. and 30 : 71 mm. London, British Museum.

From the inscriptions on these two designs for jewellery, " Well laydi well " and " Mi ladi prinsis," it is to be concluded that they were done as a commision for Henry VIII or one of his wives.

Besides pearls and precious stones, gold, silver and coloured enamel were used as materials for jewellery.

56 *Time brings Truth to Light*

Pen, brush and ink, 97 : 101 mm. Basle, Öffentliche Kunstsammlung.

An arm emerging from the clouds, through the branches of a vine, seizes the hands of a naked woman, and draws her forth from a cleft in a mountain, opening like gaping jaws. The heavenly apparition is intended to represent the arm of God bringing Truth to light.

The same allegory was treated by Holbein in a small roundel inscribed with explanatory notes, in the British Museum; there, however, the whole figure of Chronos, the God of Time, is to be seen. The essential parts of the composition are enclosed by the artist within a lightly defined quadrilateral border-line intended to indicate that the drawing was to serve an ornamental purpose. Probably it was to decorate the stem of a drinking cup.

HANS HOLBEIN D. Ä.
DIE MADONNA ALS HIMMELSKÖNIGIN

HANS HOLBEIN THE ELDER
THE VIRGIN AS QUEEN OF HEAVEN

I

HANS HOLBEIN D. Ä.
AMBROSIUS UND HANS HOLBEIN

HANS HOLBEIN THE ELDER
AMBROSIUS AND HANS HOLBEIN

HANS HOLBEIN D. Ä.
SIGMUND HOLBEIN

HANS HOLBEIN THE ELDER
SIGMUND HOLBEIN

HANS HOLBEIN D. Ä.   HANS HOLBEIN THE ELDER
SELBSTBILDNIS   SELF-PORTRAIT

3

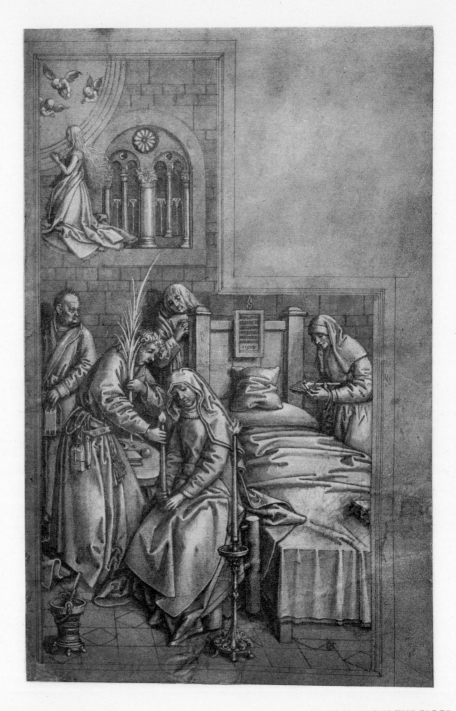

HANS HOLBEIN D. Ä.
DER TOD MARIAE

HANS HOLBEIN THE ELDER
DEATH OF THE VIRGIN

4

HANS HOLBEIN D. Ä.   HANS HOLBEIN THE ELDER
DER HEILIGE GEORG   ST. GEORGE

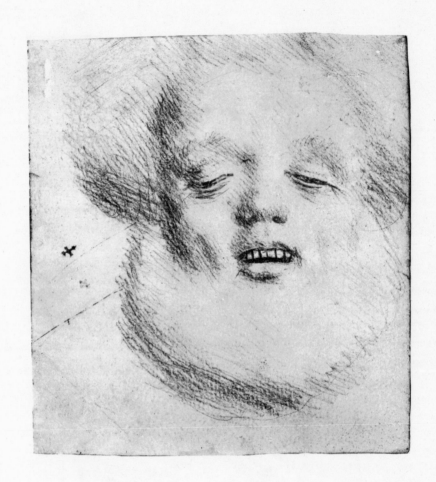

HANS HOLBEIN D. Ä.   HANS HOLBEIN THE ELDER
GREISENANTLITZ   HEAD OF AN OLD MAN

HANS HOLBEIN D. Ä.   HANS HOLBEIN THE ELDER
DER PRIOR JOHANN VON WILNAU THE PRIOR JOHANN VON WILNAU

HANS HOLBEIN D. Ä.   HANS HOLBEIN THE ELDER
JUNGES MÄDCHEN MIT OFFENEM HAAR   YOUNG GIRL WITH LONG HAIR

8

HANS HOLBEIN D. Ä.   HANS HOLBEIN THE ELDER
KNABENBILDNIS   PORTRAIT OF A BOY

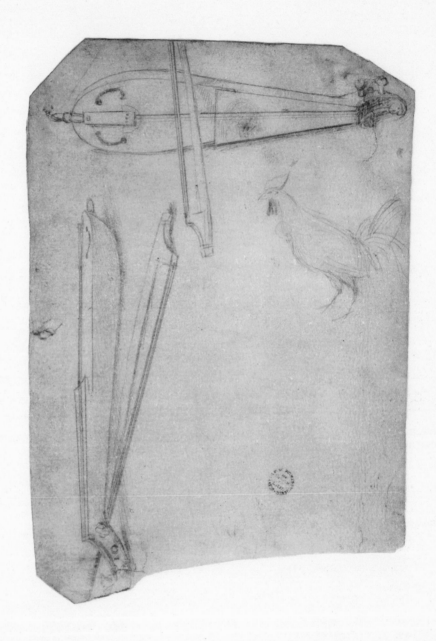

HANS HOLBEIN D. Ä.
SKIZZENBLATT

HANS HOLBEIN THE ELDER
PAGE FROM A SKETCH-BOOK

10

HANS HOLBEIN D. Ä.
HANDSTUDIEN

HANS HOLBEIN THE ELDER
STUDIES OF HAND

HANS HOLBEIN D. Ä.
DER SCHREIBMEISTER
LEONHARD WAGNER

HANS HOLBEIN THE ELDER
THE WRITING-MASTER
LEONHARD WAGNER

HANS HOLBEIN D. Ä.
ULRICH ARTZT
BÜRGERMEISTER VON AUGSBURG

HANS HOLBEIN THE ELDER
ULRICH ARTZT
BURGOMASTER OF AUGSBURG

13

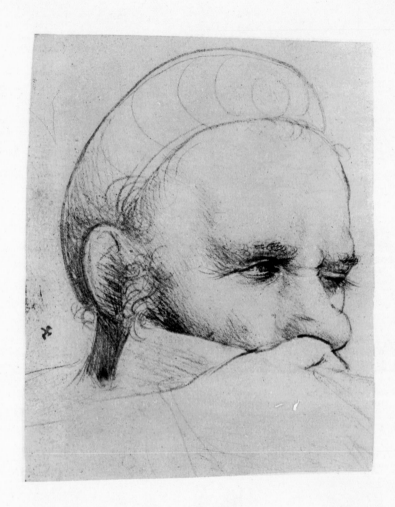

HANS HOLBEIN D. Ä.　　　　　　　　　　HANS HOLBEIN THE ELDER
ARMBRUSTSCHÜTZE　　　　　　　　　　　　　　　　AN ARCHER

HANS HOLBEIN D. Ä.   HANS HOLBEIN THE ELDER
„DER ALLE ZEYT GUTE GESEL"   A JOLLY GOOD FELLOW

AMBROSIUS HOLBEIN
KNABENBILDNIS

AMBROSIUS HOLBEIN
PORTRAIT OF A BOY

16

AMBROSIUS HOLBEIN
JÜNGLINGSBILDNIS

AMBROSIUS HOLBEIN
PORTRAIT OF A YOUTH

AMBROSIUS HOLBEIN
PYRAMUS UND THISBE

AMBROSIUS HOLBEIN
PYRAMUS AND THISBE

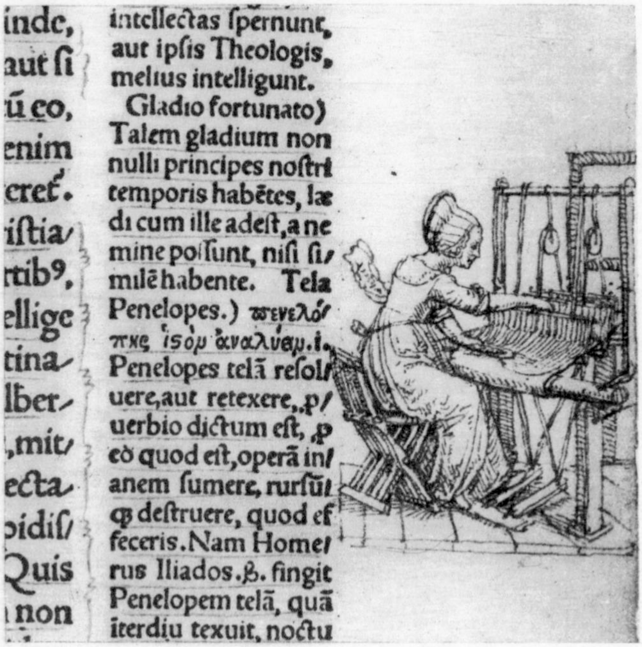

HANS HOLBEIN D. J.
PENELOPE AM WEBSTUHL

HANS HOLBEIN THE YOUNGER
PENELOPE AT HER LOOM

AMBROSIUS HOLBEIN
TOURNAMENT OF CHILDREN

AMBROSIUS HOLBEIN
KINDERTURNIER

20

HANS HOLBEIN THE YOUNGER
THE MAN OF SORROWS

HANS HOLBEIN D. J.
DER SCHMERZENSMANN

HANS HOLBEIN D. J.
JAKOB MEYER
BÜRGERMEISTER VON BASEL

HANS HOLBEIN THE YOUNGER
JACOB MEYER
BURGOMASTER OF BASEL

HANS HOLBEIN D. J.
MARIA UND JOHANNES
UNTERM KREUZ

HANS HOLBEIN THE YOUNGER
THE VIRGIN AND ST. JOHN
BESIDE THE CROSS

23

HANS HOLBEIN D. J.
WAPPEN
DES HANS FLECKENSTEIN

HANS HOLBEIN THE YOUNGER
THE COAT-OF-ARMS
OF HANS FLECKENSTEIN

HANS HOLBEIN D. J.
LEAINA VOR DEN RICHTERN

HANS HOLBEIN THE YOUNGER
LEAINA BEFORE THE JUDGES

25

HANS HOLBEIN D. J.   HANS HOLBEIN THE YOUNGER
DER HEILIGE ADRIAN   ST. ADRIAN

26

HANS HOLBEIN D. J.   HANS HOLBEIN THE YOUNGER
DIE MADONNA IN DER NISCHE   THE VIRGIN IN AN ALCOVE

HANS HOLBEIN D. J.
DER BANNERTRÄGER DES LIVINENTALS

HANS HOLBEIN THE YOUNGER
THE STANDARD-BEARER OF LIVINENTAL

HANS HOLBEIN D. J.   HANS HOLBEIN THE YOUNGER
DIE HEILIGE KUNIGUNDE   ST. KUNIGUNDA

HANS HOLBEIN D. J.
STUDIE ZUR
MADONNA VON SOLOTHURN

HANS HOLBEIN THE YOUNGER
STUDY FOR THE
MADONNA OF SOLOTHURN

30

HANS HOLBEIN D. J.   HANS HOLBEIN THE YOUNGER
DER HERZOG JEAN DE BERRY   DUC JEAN DE BERRY

HANS HOLBEIN D. J.
LEPRAKRANKER

HANS HOLBEIN THE YOUNGER
THE LEPER

HANS HOLBEIN D. J. HANS HOLBEIN THE YOUNGER
STEINWERFERIN WOMAN WITH A STONE

33

HANS HOLBEIN D. J.
REHABEAM DROHT DEN RÄTEN

HANS HOLBEIN THE YOUNGER
REHABEAM THREATENING THE COUNCILLORS

HANS HOLBEIN D. J.
ENTWURF FÜR EINE HAUSFASSADE

HANS HOLBEIN THE YOUNGER
DESIGN FOR THE FAÇADE OF A HOUSE

35

Iohn More Sᵗ Thomas Mores Son.

HANS HOLBEIN D. J.   HANS HOLBEIN THE YOUNGER
JOHN MORE   JOHN MORE

36

HANS HOLBEIN D. J.   HANS HOLBEIN THE YOUNGER
BILDNIS EINER UNBEKANNTEN   PORTRAIT OF AN UNKNOWN LADY

HANS HOLBEIN D. J.   HANS HOLBEIN THE YOUNGER
SCHWEIZERDOLCH-SCHEIDE   SWISS DAGGER SHEATH

HANS HOLBEIN D. J.   HANS HOLBEIN THE YOUNGER
DER PARNASS   PARNASSUS

HANS HOLBEIN THE YOUNGER
LAMB AND HEAD OF A LAMB

HANS HOLBEIN D. J.
LAMM UND KOPF EINES LAMMES

40

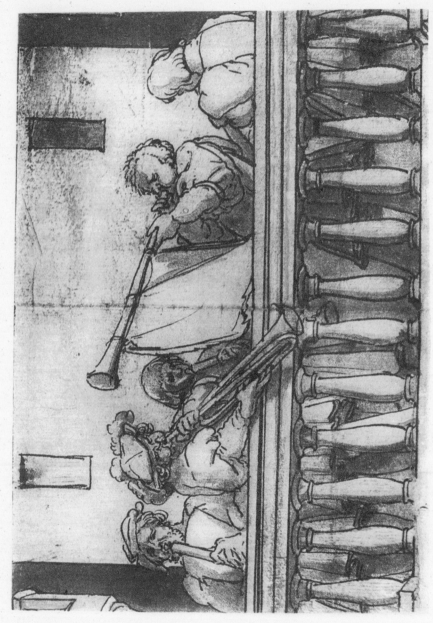

HANS HOLBEIN D. J.
FÜNF BLÄSER AUF EINER GALERIE

HANS HOLBEIN THE YOUNGER
FIVE TRUMPETERS IN A GALLERY

HANS HOLBEIN D. J.
DIE SCHÖNE PHYLLIS

HANS HOLBEIN THE YOUNGER
THE FAIR PHYLLIS

42

HANS HOLBEIN D. J.
KOSTÜMSTUDIE

HANS HOLBEIN THE YOUNGER
STUDY OF COSTUME

HANS HOLBEIN D. J.   HANS HOLBEIN THE YOUNGER
BILDNIS EINER UNBEKANNTEN   PORTRAIT OF AN UNKNOWN LADY

HANS HOLBEIN D. J.
JOHN FISHER
BISCHOF VON ROCHESTER

HANS HOLBEIN THE YOUNGER
JOHN FISHER
BISHOP OF ROCHESTER

45

HANS HOLBEIN D. J. HANS HOLBEIN THE YOUNGER
SELBSTBILDNIS SELF-PORTRAIT

46

HANS HOLBEIN D. J.   HANS HOLBEIN THE YOUNGER
BILDNIS EINES UNBEKANNTEN   PORTRAIT OF AN UNKNOWN MAN

47

The Lady Henegham.

HANS HOLBEIN D. J.
LADY HENEGHAM

HANS HOLBEIN THE YOUNGER
THE LADY HENEGHAM

48

HANS HOLBEIN D. J.   HANS HOLBEIN THE YOUNGER
BILDNIS EINER UNBEKANNTEN   PORTRAIT OF AN UNKNOWN LADY

49

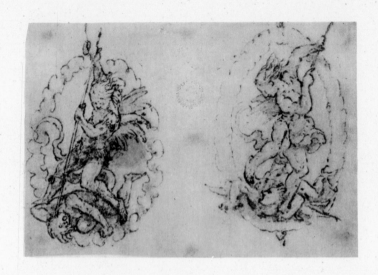

HANS HOLBEIN D. J.   HANS HOLBEIN THE YOUNGER
DREI ENTWÜRFE FÜR ORDEN   THREE DESIGNS FOR DECORATIONS

HANS HOLBEIN D. J.
SPIEGELRAHMEN
MIT MEERWEIB UND AMORETTEN

HANS HOLBEIN THE YOUNGER
MIRROR FRAME
WITH MERMAID AND CUPIDS

HANS HOLBEIN D. J.　　　　　　　　　　　　HANS HOLBEIN THE YOUNGER
ENTWURF ZU EINEM TAFELAUFSATZ　　　　　DESIGN FOR A TABLE ORNAMENT

52

HANS HOLBEIN D. J.
ENTWURF ZU EINEM DECKELPOKAL

HANS HOLBEIN THE YOUNGER
DESIGN FOR A COVERED GOBLET

53

HANS HOLBEIN D. J.   HANS HOLBEIN THE YOUNGER
PRINZ EDUARD VON WALES   EDWARD, PRINCE OF WALES
TANTALUS   TANTALUS

54

HANS HOLBEIN D. J.   HANS HOLBEIN THE YOUNGER
ENTWÜRFE FÜR SCHMUCKSTÜCKE   DESIGNS FOR JEWELLERY

HANS HOLBEIN D. J.
DIE ZEIT BRINGT
DIE WAHRHEIT AN DEN TAG

HANS HOLBEIN THE YOUNGER
TIME BRINGS
TRUTH TO LIGHT